Native American Crafts

of the Northeast and Southeast

By Judith Hoffman Corwin

Franklin Watts

A Division of Scholastic Inc.

New York Toronto London Auckland Sydney
Mexico City New Delhi Hong Kong
Danbury, Connecticut

For Jules Arthur and Oliver Jamie,
and for the makers of these wondrous and beautiful things,
who, through the ages, in many different ways, paint, sculpt,
and sing of the Earth.

I would also like to thank my editor, Lorna Greenberg, for all her
generous help, support, and cheerful spirit.

Book design by A. Natacha Pimentel C.

Library of Congress Cataloging-in-Publication Data
Corwin, Judith Hoffman.
        Native American crafts of the Northeast and Southeast / by Judith
    Hoffman Corwin.
            p. cm.
        Includes index.
        ISBN 0-531-12200-X (lib. bdg.)   0-531-15593-5 (pbk.)
        1. Indian craft—Juvenile literature. 2. Indians of North America—
Industries—Northeastern States—Juvenile literature. 3. Indians of North America—
Industries—Southern States—Juvenile literature. I. Title.
TT22 .C65 2002
745'.089974—dc21   2002005301

Contents

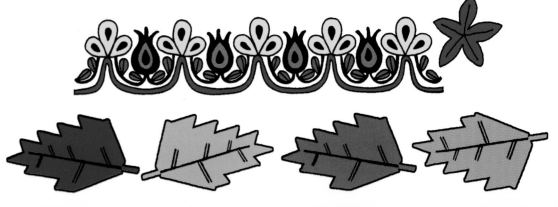

About the Native American Crafts Books

We are half in this world and half in the spirit world.
We are like the trees that have one part above the ground
and an equal part out of sight beneath the surface.

—Fox

Native Americans are believed to have been the first people to arrive on the North American continent thousands of years ago. They developed rich cultures based on their respect for the natural world around them—the Earth, sky, wind, rain, animals, plants, fire and water, the sun, the moon, and the stars.

The spirit of nature is important to Native Americans, and the design and decoration of the objects they use in their daily lives—to raise families, to farm, to hunt, to defend themselves or to make war—reflect the elements of nature. The designs on their clothing, pottery, baskets, dwellings, and weapons are decorative and are also an appeal to the goodwill of the spirits of the natural world. Native American people have no word for art because creating art is an integral part of life.

Now many Native Americans live in cities. Yet they often return to their home reservations to visit families and for special occasions. Their past is kept alive through storytelling and through arts and crafts. Traditional crafts, like the stories, are handed down from generation to generation, carrying along a cultural message.

The Native American Crafts series of books introduces young people to the cultures of Native Americans and to their creative work. We can learn about and appreciate Native American culture and incorporate what we learn into our lives through making art objects inspired by their examples. The projects in these books are based on crafts of everyday life, but do not involve ritual or religious objects. ◈

Native Americans of the Northeast and Southeast

Hundreds of years ago, Native Americans in what is now the Northeast and Southeast regions of the United States lived amid beautiful forests with abundant wildlife and fresh water. The fertile land supported many different groups of people.

The Northeast

The Algonquians were a large group of tribes united by language. They included the Ojibwa (Chippewa), Fox, Sauk, Shawnee, Mohegan, Delaware, Abnaki, Massachusetts, and Micmac tribes. They were scattered through a region from the Atlantic Ocean to the Rocky Mountains. The Iroquois—an alliance that included the Mohawk, Onondaga, Oneida, Cayuga, and Seneca tribes—made up another large group. They lived in areas from the Atlantic Coast to Lake Erie, and from Ontario south into North Carolina. These forest dwellers were sometimes called the Woodland People.

NORTH AMERICA

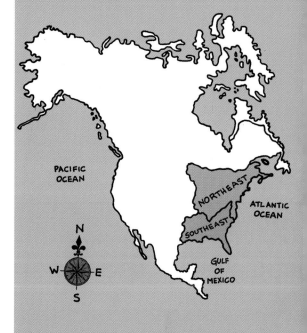

The Algonquian homelands provided everything for the people. The soil was fertile for farming, and the woods and streams provided wildlife for food and clothing. Villages consisted of wigwams constructed of bent tree limbs covered with skins, woven mats, evergreen boughs, or birchbark. When the village moved, the covering was rolled up and saved to use again. Algonquian men hunted fox, rabbit, beaver, deer, and moose. Men and women fished with spears, nets, or traps. Women made clothing and wove fishnets and mats. They gathered roots, nuts, and berries and collected sap to make maple sugar. Some tribes raised corn, beans, squash, and melons.

The Iroquois called themselves "we who are of the extended lodge." Their homes were large bark and wood longhouses that could hold many families. They lived mostly by hunting and fishing, and grew a few crops, especially corn, beans, and squash—the "three sisters."

The Southeast

Southeastern Native Americans lived in an area from the Atlantic Ocean west to what is now eastern Oklahoma, and northward from the Gulf of Mexico to the southern Appalachian Mountains and down into Florida. Southeastern people included the Cherokee, Creek, Natchez, Choctaw, Caddo, and Seminole.

Some Woodland People, like the Seminole, lived farther south, in the Florida Everglades and the Big Cypress Swamp. Their traditional houses—chickees—were built on stilts high above the swampy ground; their thatched roofs and open sides let in cool breezes. Seminole women raised corn, beans, and squash and collected grapes, plums, and figs. The men fished and hunted deer, bear, turkeys, alligators, and other animals. ◆

Here's What You Need:
- paints, brushes, colored pencils or markers
- paper, T-shirts, cotton fabric, clay, or other materials as needed

Northeast and Southeast Designs and Symbols

Native American art and decoration is filled with creative energy. Everyday objects are made handsome to show appreciation to the Great Spirit, the giver of all things. Many designs are linked to nature. They remind us of plants, animals, the landscape, the skies, and the weather. You can paint the designs on T-shirts, greeting cards, and stationery or etch them on clay bowls or tablets. You can use them for jewelry or on murals, scrolls, bookmarks, or book covers. ◆

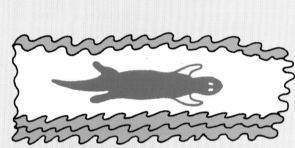

- For stamped designs, ask an adult to help you use the knife. Cut a potato in half. Draw a design on the cut surface of one half. Cut away the background about 1/4 inch (6 mm) deep. Pour a little paint onto a piece of aluminum foil. Press the stamp into the paint and then onto the basket. Repeat as many times as you wish. You can make another stamp and decorate the basket with two designs.

Here's What You Need:
- pencil, ruler, scissors, glue
- 7 by 14 inch (18 by 35 cm) piece of felt or heavy fabric
- fine-line marker, permanent colored markers
- long shoelace or 20 inch (50 cm) piece of rope

Here's How You Do It:
- Fold the fabric in half. With a pencil, draw the outline of the pouch. To allow for a fringe, add 2 inches (5 cm) along the sides and the bottom. Cut out the pouch. You will have two pieces—one for the back and one for the front of the pouch. On each piece, cut six slits 1-1/2 inches (3.8 cm) from the top edge.
- Draw designs on both pieces with fine-line markers. Color in the designs with permanent markers.

Woodland Pouch

Native American people make pouches and bags to hold everyday items or ceremonial objects. They are usually made of animal skin and decorated with traditional designs. Woodland people often use floral designs. We will make a decorated Woodland pouch.

16

- With scissors, cut fringes along the sides and the bottom. Place the front piece facedown and squeeze out a thin line of glue along the sides and bottom edge. Press the front and back pieces together and let them dry.
- Thread a shoelace or a length of rope through the slits. Make knots at each end. Pull the two ends to close the pouch.

17

Here's What You Need:
- cardboard, pencil, scissors
- glue, rope, stapler
- dried cornhusks or tan crepe paper

Here's How You Do It:
- On a piece of cardboard, draw an oval shape at least as large as your face. Cut it out.
- Draw holes for eyes and the mouth. Cut out the holes.
- Glue lengths of rope to the cardboard. Glue another layer of rope in a circle around each eye and around the mouth.
- Build up a nose with strips of rope.
- Cut the dried cornhusks or crepe paper into 3-inch (8-cm) long strips. Glue the ends to the back of the mask to look like hair.
- Staple lengths of rope to the sides of the mask at eye level. Use them to tie on the mask.

Iroquois Cornhusk Mask

The Iroquois people make special masks for celebrations to give thanks for bountiful harvests and the gift of corn. Cornhusk Face Messengers run through the village ahead of False Face Dancers. The Cornhusk Face Messengers represent the agricultural spirits who taught people to grow crops. The masks are made of dried cornhusks that have been woven into cord. The cord is fashioned into a mask with eyeholes and a mouthhole. The nose and cheeks are raised and strips of dried corn stalks are attached for hair. We will make a mask using rope. These beautiful masks can be worn or hung on a wall.

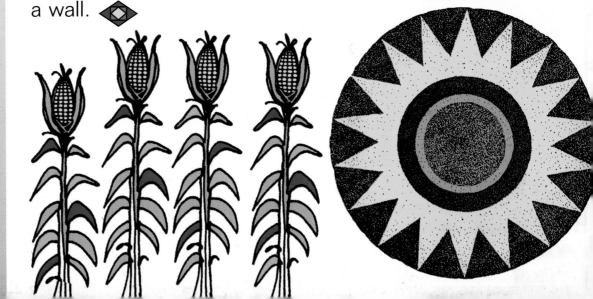

19

Here's What You Need:
- homemade clay (page 47)
- pencil, paints, brushes
- glue, yarn or cord, buttons or beads

Here's How You Do It:
- Pinch off a piece of clay (page 47) as big as a tennis ball and shape the turtle's body. Pinch off six small pieces of clay to make a head, legs, and a tail. Shape and attach these to the body.
- Adjust the head so that the turtle is looking up. With the point of a pencil, carve a mouth and lines to show toes.
- Bake the clay turtle (page 47). Let it cool.
- Paint the turtle's shell. Draw on symbols for the sun, water, moon, lightning, and a star. Paint the head and tail.
- Glue some buttons or beads to the shell, or string them on a piece of yarn or cord and tie it around the shell.

Great Turtle Sculpture

Many moons ago, when the Earth was covered by water, Great Turtle ruled over all the animals. One day, Great Turtle saw a tree and a woman fall from the sky into the water. Two swans swam to rescue the woman. Great Turtle ordered otter, beaver, and muskrat to dive into the water and bring up the soil surrounding the tree's roots. They tried, but none could do this. Finally, toad brought up some mud and placed it on Great Turtle's back. The mud was magical: it grew larger and larger and formed an island. The swans placed the woman upon Great Turtle Island, which continued to grow until it became our world. We will make a clay sculpture of the Great Turtle of this Iroquois story.

TOP VIEW

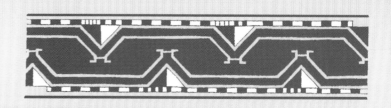

Here's What You Need:
- homemade clay (page 47)
- poster or acrylic paints, brushes, newspaper, fine-line markers
- 4- by 3-inch (10- by 7.6-cm) piece of white fabric, glue
- pencil, scissors, 1-1/2 by 3 inch (3.8 by 7.6 cm) piece of cardboard
- colored markers
- strips of 1/2-inch (1.2-cm) wide ribbon or brown cloth

Here's How You Do It:
- Pull off a handful of clay (page 47) and shape it into a small head and body.
- Paint the head and body. If you use acrylic paint, protect your work surfaces with newspaper. When dry, use a fine-line marker to draw the eyes, nose, mouth, and hair.

Micmac Baby and Cradleboard

Native Americans used cradleboards to hold small babies and transport them. Women carried a cradleboard in their arms or strapped it to their backs. The boards could be slung from saddles, hung from a tree branch, or rested against a rock while the mothers picked berries or worked in the fields. A hoop protected the baby if the cradleboard tipped over. Our cradleboard will hold an infant doll wrapped in a blanket.

- Wrap the baby in the blanket—the white fabric. Fold over a collar around the face. Glue the side edges together. Fold the bottom edge under and glue it closed at the back of the baby. With markers, draw designs on the blanket.
- Draw the cradleboard on the cardboard. Cut it out, making the top corners round. Paint and decorate the back of the board.
- Glue the wrapped baby to the cradleboard. Tie ribbon strips around the baby and board.

Here's What You Need:
- homemade clay (page 47)
- table knife, pencil
- poster or acrylic paints and brushes, or paint markers, newspaper to protect work surface
- glue, string, or yarn

Here's How You Do It:
- Set aside a walnut-sized lump of clay. Roll and pat out the rest to the size of a dinner plate. It should be about 1/4 inch (6 mm) thick. Shape it into a face with a pointed chin.
- Shape the set-aside clay into a coil or small snake. Place this on the mask and shape it into a bent nose. With a pencil, draw creases on the forehead and make a hole at each side. With a knife, cut out the eyes and mouth.
- Bake the mask (page 47). When it is cool, paint it. Draw on designs. Glue on string or yarn for hair. Attach strings at the side holes to tie on the mask.

False Face Mask

Among the Iroquois, healing ceremonies were performed by a society of masked men who drew power from the trees. To make a mask, each man would find a basswood tree. After saying prayers and asking the tree to share its healing power, the person carved a face into the tree trunk. Then he cut the face away from the tree—carefully, so the tree was not harmed. A typical mask has a twisted nose and mouth because of an Iroquois legend about two brothers, Great Spirit and Evil Spirit, who created all things on Earth. Great Spirit made good things, such as forests, mountains, and valleys. Evil Spirit brought danger and sickness. The brothers held a contest to see who could move a mountain. Evil Spirit went first. Concentrating his powers, he moved the mountain slightly, then turned to see his brother's reaction. But at that moment, Great Spirit quietly slid the mountain right up to his brother's face. When Evil Spirit turned back, he smashed his face on the rock and bent his nose. Although the bad things that Evil Spirit made still trouble us, the mask reminds us that life also holds many good things.

Here's What You Need:
- white fabric (an old sheet or other material), or felt
- scissors, pencil, colored fabric markers

Here's How You Do It:
- Trace and transfer (page 46) or copy the designs you want to use onto the fabric. Use a long strip for a belt or sash, or a 4- by 12-inch (10- by 30-cm) piece for a bookmark.
- Go over the lines with fabric markers. Color in the designs.
- With scissors, cut slits to make fringed edges.

Wampum Design Belt and Bookmark

The Woodland People recorded peace treaties, good fortune, and other important happenings by weaving symbols and pictures into bead-covered bands called wampum belts. Wampum beads, which are purple or white, were made from clamshells or other shells. Native Americans cut the shells and drilled holes in them with stone tools. They rubbed the beads with sand to polish them.

We will make a belt or sash, or a bookmark, with wampum-style designs. Some traditional designs are figures holding hands (friendship), diagonal lines (a message, or support for a treaty), parallel lines (paths or trails), outlined crosses (territories or nations), a deer, a thunderbird, lightning, a peace belt, and a panther.

FRIENDSHIP

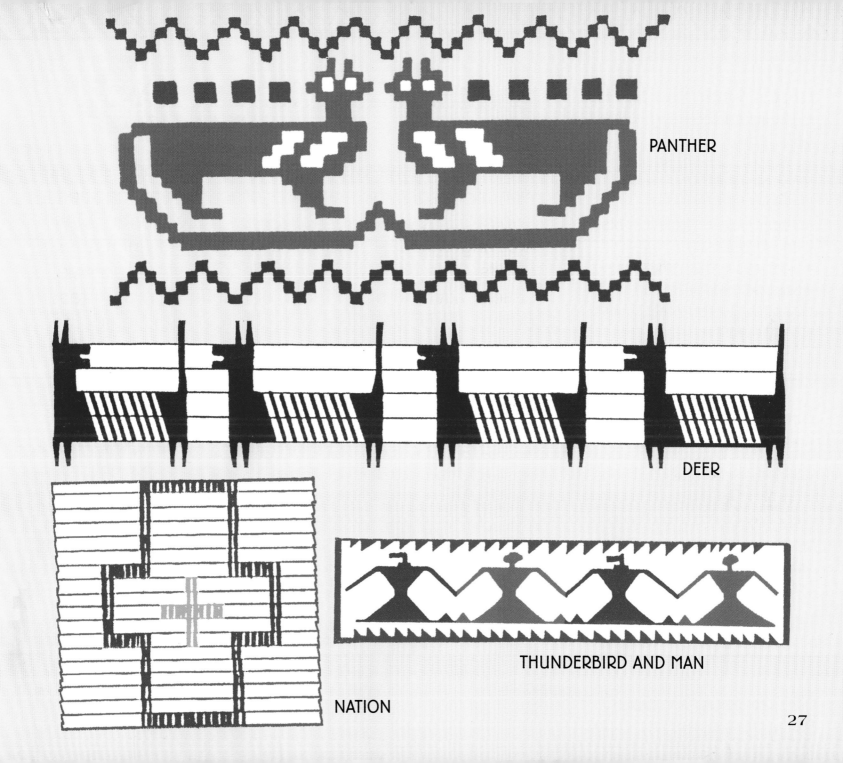

PANTHER

DEER

NATION

THUNDERBIRD AND MAN

27

Here's What You Need:
- crumpled tissues or cotton balls, string
- 12-inch (30-cm) square piece of white or tan fabric, needle and thread
- beads, paint, brushes, black yarn, glue, scissors
- colored or patterned fabric; rickrack, braid, or ribbon
- 5 inch (13 cm) plate, 7 inch (18 cm) plate

Here's How You Do It:
- For the doll's head, put two crumpled tissues or four cotton balls in the center of the fabric square. Tie a string below the tissues to form the neck.
- Stuff in more tissues or cotton balls below the neck to make a body. Sew the bottom of the body closed. Traditional dolls have no arms or legs.

Seminole Doll

Native American women of the Southeast usually wore skirts, and the men wore loincloths and leggings. In winter, they draped cloak-like "matchcoats" over their shoulders. These were made from animal fur, grasses, or bark, and were decorated with animal designs, geometric patterns, or paintings of important events. Their clothing was colored with vegetable dyes or painted with mineral paints. We will make a Seminole doll and dress it in traditional woman's clothing. ◈

28

- Sew on black beads for eyes, or paint them on. Paint on eyebrows, a nose, and a red mouth. Glue on black yarn for hair, or paint it on.
- Put the smaller plate on the colored fabric and draw around it. Cut out this circle and cut a small hole in the center. Pull the circle down over the doll's head for a blouse. Gather it around the neck with a few stitches.
- Use the larger plate to draw a circle for the skirt. Cut it out and cut a hole in the center. Slip it onto the doll's waist and sew it on. Glue rickrack, braid, or ribbon around the blouse and skirt.
- String beads on a thread and tie it around the doll's neck. Sew or glue on bead earrings.

Here's What You Need:
- 7-inch (18-cm) by 16-inch (40-cm) piece of fake leather, Ultrasuede, chamois cloth, felt, or other heavy fabric
- pencil, scissors, hole punch or nail
- strips of leather or string, beads, rope, glue
- acrylic or poster paints and brushes or permanent markers, newspaper

Here's How You Do It:
- With a pencil, draw the outline of the bag on the fabric. Cut it out. Make the top corners round.
- Fold the bottom third of the cloth up to make the bag. The top third will be folded down later for a flap.
- With a nail or a hole punch, make holes on each side of the bag. Thread leather strips or strings through the holes to make tassels. Thread a few beads onto the ends of the tassels and secure them with a knot.

30

Friendship Bag

Native Americans used bags for things they needed to carry, such as flints and steel to make fire. Some bags were called "friendship bags" because people filled them with gifts when they went visiting. We will make a decorated friendship bag like those used by the Woodland tribes.

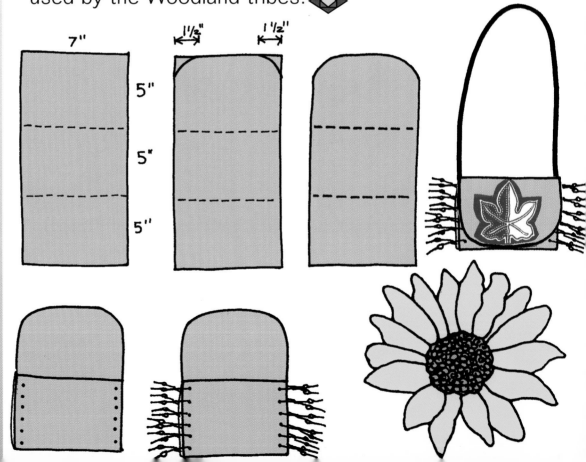

- Cut off a 36-inch (91-cm) length of rope for a shoulder strap. Punch out two holes at the top of the bag, each about 1 inch (2.5 cm) in from the side edge. Pull the rope through the hole on one side. Make a large knot to hold it. Pull the other end of the rope through the hole on the other side. Make a large knot. Fold down the flap.
- Draw a design on the bag below the flap and color it in. Draw designs on the back of the bag and the flap. If you use acrylic paint, cover your work surfaces with newspaper.

31

Here's What You Need:
- 3-inch (7.6-cm) square of heavy felt or fabric, pen, ruler
- round button, glue, scissors
- seed beads (from a craft store) in red, white, blue, and green
- thread or dental floss, needle, shoelace

Here's How You Do It:
- With a pen and ruler, draw diagonal lines from each corner of the square. They will cross at the center of the square. Glue the button down on the center point.
- Cut a length of thread (or dental floss, if the needle is large enough). Pull one end through the needle and knot the ends together. Push the needle into the underside of the felt, close to the button, and draw it up through the felt.
- String several red beads onto the needle. Push the needle down through the felt and then bring it back up, pulling the thread tight. Repeat until you have made a circle around the button.

Beaded Rosette

The rosette, or circle, is a symbol of the cycle of life, or the yearly cycle of seasons. Native Americans use the rosette to decorate clothing, horses, pouches, and more. Your rosette can be a decorative patch on a bag, jacket, or jeans, or a hair band or cap. Or follow the instructions to make it into a necklace. ◆

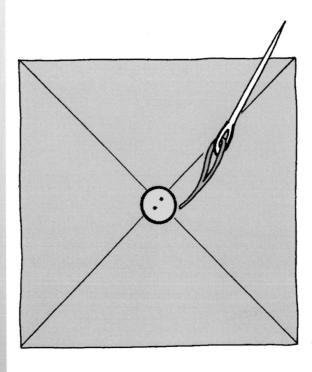

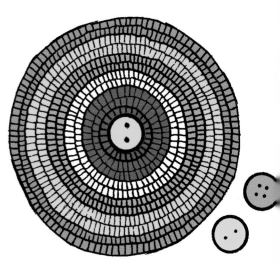

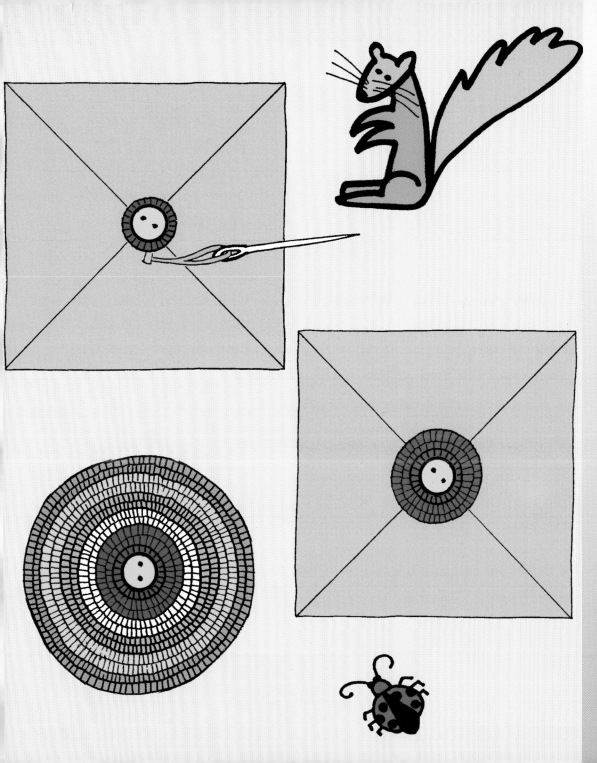

- Start a new circle by bringing the needle up half a bead's width outside the first circle. String on six beads. Push the needle down through the felt near the end of the first circle. Come back up between the third and fourth beads of the new circle.
- Thread the needle through the last three beads. Sew on another circle of red beads.
- After three circles of red beads, sew on two circles of white, then blue, then yellow, and then green. Make your bead circles close together.
- At the end of the last circle, push the needle through the first bead to sew it down. Knot the thread on the underside of the felt. Cut off the needle. With scissors, trim the felt along the edges of the circle.
- To make a necklace, use a shoelace long enough to go around your neck, plus several inches. Fold it in half to find the center. Sew on the rosette at this spot. Make a knot and cut off the needle. Tie the ends of the lace together.

Here's What You Need:
- white paper, pencil, card-board or oaktag, ruler
- colored paper or felt, or white paper and colored markers
- scissors, glue stick

Here's How You Do It:
- One way to make patch-work designs is to draw the designs on white paper with a pencil. Color them in with markers.
- Another way is to draw the designs on paper, oaktag, cardboard, or heavy fabric, then glue on cut-up pieces of felt or colored paper.

Seminole Patchwork

In the early 1900s, Native American women in the Florida Everglades developed a style of patchwork, using cotton fabric. We will make a patchwork design out of colored paper or felt or out of white paper painted with markers. Here are several designs; the diamond shape represents a rattlesnake. You can create your own design. Use these designs as borders for stationary, or glue them onto cardboard to make picture frames.

RATTLESNAKE

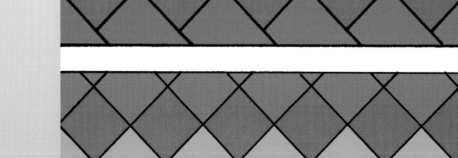

34

Water Spider Legend

In Cherokee legend, in the beginning, the world had no fire. It was cold. Then Thunder sent Lightning to put fire into a hollow tree. But the tree was on an island, so it could not be reached. Finally, Water Spider spun a thread and wove it into a bowl. With more thread, she tied the bowl onto her back. She swam to the island, took a burning coal from the fire and put it into her bowl. Then she swam back, carrying fire to people.

In ancient times, the Cherokee used stone tools to carve the legend of Water Spider onto a large conch shell. They made black paint from burned plants and rubbed some into the lines of the drawing to make it stand out. We will draw Water Spider on a rock. You can also draw other ancient designs—a bird and a winged serpent (page 10).

(page 10)

Here's What You Need:
* smooth rock large enough for the spider drawing
* pencil, tracing paper
* black fine-line permanent marker

Here's How You Do It:
* Trace and transfer (page 46) the design onto your rock, or draw it freehand.
* Go over the pencil lines with a fine-line black permanent marker.

(page 46)

Here's What You Need:
- pencil, heavyweight paper, scissors
- fine-line black and colored markers

Here's How You Do It:
- Press your hand down on a sheet of paper and draw around it with a pencil. Cut it out.
- Choose designs from those shown here or on pages 10-13 to tell a story.
- Draw the designs on the paper hand. Color in the designs.

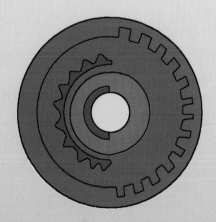

Storytelling Hand

You can use Native American designs and symbols to tell a story of an adventure, of your day in the country, or anything else. Use your landscape—the trees, the flowers, the sky, and the animals and insects around you—to decorate your own hand shape.

Porcupine Quill Box

The porcupine is a sharp-toothed rodent whose body is covered with spear-like quills. Woodland People use the white quills with black tips to decorate objects such as birchbark boxes. To get quills, a blanket or animal skin is thrown over the animal, which then releases hundreds of quills to defend itself. The quills are softened in water, then flattened and dyed. Next, they are wrapped, woven, or sewn onto the object. We will decorate a box using toothpicks as porcupine quills.

Here's What You Need:
- tracing paper, pencil
- small solid-color box of wood or cardboard
- black fine-line marker, colored markers
- glue, black beads, toothpicks, scissors

Here's How You Do It:
- Trace and transfer (page 46) the porcupine design onto the box. Draw over the lines with a black fine-line marker. Glue on black beads for eyes.
- With scissors, cut the toothpicks into 1 inch (2.5 cm) pieces. Glue some pieces onto the animal's back and tail. Add some for whiskers. Cut some 1/4 inch (6 cm) pieces and glue them on for claws. Color the nose black and draw the ears.

• To make the star designs, color some 1-inch (2.5-cm) toothpick pieces red, yellow, and blue. When dry, glue them around the porcupine to form a border. You can use the box to store treasures.

Chief Sunflower

The woodlands are full of flowers. The sunflower, the largest, is the "chief" of the flower world. We will grow sunflowers in a windowsill garden.

Here's What You Need:
- pencil, stick, or nail
- sunflower seeds (available at hardware stores, garden stores, or in catalogues)
- earth or potting soil
- four yogurt cups or other containers, saucers
- four empty coffee cans, saucers
- four large flowerpots or plastic containers
- large spoon, watering can or pitcher, sticks, rags

Here's How You Do It:
- You need a sunny windowsill. In early May or June, punch a few drainage holes in the bottom of the yogurt cups or containers. Fill them half-way with soil. Put the cups on saucers to catch leakage. Push three or four seeds into the soil in each container. Cover them with a thin layer of soil. Water the seeds whenever the soil seems dry.

- Ask an adult to punch drainage holes in the coffee cans. When the seedlings are 2 inches (5 cm) high, gently transplant them with their soil to the cans. Add more soil if needed. Place saucers underneath.

- When the plants are 4 inches (10 cm) high, transfer them into large plastic containers or large flowerpots. Ask an adult to make drainage holes in these containers and place trays or pans underneath them.

- Sunflowers grow quickly and need support. Push a strong stick into the soil near each plant and tie the stalk to it with a rag. Water your plants when necessary and watch them grow. They can reach 6 feet (1.8 m) in height and the flowers can be 12 inches (30 cm) around.

Sunflower Seed Snack

Dried sunflower seeds make a tasty snack or granola-type cereal.

Here's What You Need:
- 3-1/2 cups rolled oats
- 1/2 cup unprocessed wheat bran
- 1 cup sunflower seeds
- 1/2 cup chopped almonds
- 1/4 cup sesame oil
- 1/2 teaspoon salt
- 1 teaspoon vanilla extract
- 1 cup chopped dates
- 1 cup raisins
- mixing bowl and spoon, spatula
- cookie sheet, aluminum foil, potholders, jar with lid

Here's How You Do It:
- Ask an adult to help you preheat the oven to 325° F. (165° C.).
- In a bowl, combine all the ingredients except the raisins and dates. Cover the cookie sheet with aluminum foil. Spread the mixture on the sheet.
- Bake for 15 minutes. Using potholders, remove the cookie sheet. Stir the mixture and bake for 15 minutes more. Remove from the oven. When the mixture is cool, pour it into a bowl and add the raisins and dates. Store it in a tightly covered container.

43

Here's What You Need:
- heavyweight paper
- black fine-line marker, colored markers, or pencils

Here's How You Do It:
- Select a poem and write it out on a sheet of paper with a fine-line marker.
- Make a border or add decorations using designs from this book. Color them with markers or colored pencils.

Native American Writings

Native American writings preserve many of the legends and customs of the past. Here is a small collection of poems, songs, and other works adapted from traditional Native American pieces. Through them we can learn about Native American life in the Northeast and Southeast.

We do not like to harm the trees. Whenever we can, we make an offering of food before we cut them down. We never waste the wood, but use all that we cut. If we did not think of their feelings, and did not offer them food before cutting them down, all the other trees in the forest would weep, and that would make our hearts sad too.

—Fox

Nanabush [a Native American spirit] *could change to whatever form he wanted at any time. To help animals, he became an animal. To help people, he became a person.*

—Chippewa

The Earth hears you,
The sky
And wood mountains see you.
If you believe this,
You will grow old.

—Fox

Being born as humans to this Earth
is a sacred trust. We have a sacred
responsibility. We have a special gift,
which is beyond the fine gifts of the
plants, the fish, the woodlands, the
birds, and all other living things on
Earth. We are able to take care
of them.

—Onondaga

Birds are important.
They go where they wish.
They are carefree.
We take their feathers
And use them in our ceremonies.
The eagle flies highest
Of all the birds in the sky.
His feathers are the most sacred.

—Seminole

Watch the piles of bubbles.
Friend turtle must be near.
The turtle swims with his
Head held high.
The turtle swims with a
Song in his ear.
The song is the sound
Of the river.

—Delaware

I see another sun.
It is good.
Humans make but little,
They think they know much.
All things declare
I cannot make myself.
They declare
Humans cannot make a tree.
That is so.

—Mohegan

Basic Techniques

Tracing Designs

Here's What You Need:
- tracing paper
- pencil, tape
- drawing paper, fabric, or other material

Here's How You Do It:
- Place tracing paper over the design you want to trace. If you like, tape the paper down. Trace the lines of the design, pressing firmly on your pencil.
- Remove the tape and turn the paper over. On the back, draw over the lines of the design with the side of your pencil point.
- Turn the tracing paper right side up and place it on a sheet of drawing paper or the material for your project. You may tape this down. Draw over the lines. This will transfer the design onto the paper or the material.

Making Clay

Here's What You Need:
- 2 cups flour plus extra flour to sprinkle on the work surface
- 1 cup salt
- 1 cup water
- large bowl, spoon, measuring cup
- cookie sheet, potholders, aluminum foil

Here's How You Do It:
- Use this recipe to make clay for projects in this book. Additional instructions are given with the specific projects.
- Mix the flour and salt in a bowl. Add the water a little at a time. Mix the clay well with your hands until it is smooth. The clay is ready to roll out and cut, or to shape according to the project directions.
- If you need to bake the clay, ask an adult to help you use the oven. Heat the oven to 325° F. (165° C.). Line a cookie sheet with aluminum foil and place the clay pieces on it, spacing them 1 inch (2.5 cm) apart. Bake until lightly browned, 15 to 20 minutes, but check often to see that the edges are not burning.
- Using potholders, remove the cookie sheet from the oven. Allow the clay to cool. Paint or decorate it following the project instructions.

Index